**MARTIN LUTHER SAID:**

"I am much afraid that universities will prove to be the great gates of hell, unless they diligently labor in explaining the Holy Scriptures, and engraving them in the hearts of youth. I advise no one to place his child where the Scriptures do not reign paramount. Every institution in which men are not unceasingly occupied with the Word of God must become corrupt."

# MARTIN LUTHER

by MAY McNEER and LYND WARD

New York     ABINGDON PRESS     *Nashville*

# CONTENTS

# A MINER'S SON

From cold German mountains a chill wind whipped down on the town of Eisleben. It rattled the red tiles on the roofs of houses that leaned over narrow streets. It sent strong townsmen scurrying indoors to their warm firesides.

The wind whistled as it snatched at the cloaks of a little group of people coming from the church. But the man who held a baby in his arms clasped the coverlets closer about it, and smiled proudly.

This was November 11, 1483. Only the night before the child had been born, the first son to Margaret and Hans Luther. Hans Luther and his friends carried the baby homeward, bending their heads against the wind. As the heavy door slammed shut behind them, Hans went upstairs and laid the baby beside his wife.

"His name be Martin, Margaret, for he was baptised on the day of St. Martin."

" 'Tis good, husband. And may St. Martin care for him all his life long."

Hans returned to the fire downstairs. There he sat long with his friends, rejoicing in the birth of his son. Margaret looked at the sleeping child and wondered what he would be in the world.

Hans and Margaret were humble folk. Hans came from a family of free farmers. His father owned a small farm, and the sons could move freely from place to place. They were better off than the serfs, who were bound by law to stay on the land of certain nobles and work for them without pay. But, though free, the Luthers were poor. Hans had left his father's farm to come to Eisleben to work in the coal mines. Probably this child, Martin, would some day go down into the mines also, his mother thought as she looked at him. Yet — "who knows what the good God may have in store for him," she murmured.

The wind shook the roof tiles as if it would tear the house apart. It moaned and whistled and sounded like an evil witch from the wild mountains, reaching for the babe. Margaret drew him closer, crossed herself, and prayed. Like all the people around her, she believed in witches, fairies, and gnomes. But she was a religious woman, too. Tomorrow she would take a coin from her small box and pay it to the priest for a special prayer to St. Martin.

When Martin was six months old, his parents piled their few pieces of furniture in a cart and set out for Mansfeld. Hans was not making as much money as he had hoped in the mines at Eisleben. "Maybe the mines at Mansfeld will yield better, wife," he said. "We can but try."

In the little town near the mines the Luthers found a small house. Hans worked hard, digging ore and carrying it to the smelting furnaces. Margaret labored at the endless household tasks of caring for a growing family. There was seldom enough in the house to feed them all well, as Martin's brothers and sisters arrived.

Martin played with the babies and helped his mother. He

6

often went with her to the forest to gather wood. At twilight he trudged along the road behind her, his arms piled with bundles of sticks. Margaret's back was bent low under the heavy load of fagots.

Hans came in each night, his face black from coal dust. He washed in a basin on the kitchen steps. Then he sat down with the family to eat black bread and boiled peas and to drink whey. Sometimes, on a special day, he slowly cut a wedge of cheese or a piece of sausage into thin slices. Then he handed each child a slice on the point of his knife. He smiled a little as he saw each pair of eager eyes fixed on the slow-moving knife.

After supper Martin perched on a low stool to listen to his father. Hans Luther sat, mug of beer in hand, his stocky legs close to the small fire, and talked of the news he had heard.

Martin began school when he was seven. He went to a cathedral school some distance from his home. At first he was carried on the shoulders of an older boy. He rode proudly like a knight on a horse. But Martin soon found that school was not a happy place. Here a few boys had to sit in a dark, cold, and dirty room, doing the bidding of a teacher who did not care whether the boys learned or not.

The priests themselves did not like to teach. They hired wandering university students to teach for them. The pay was so small that it scarcely provided food for the teachers. But they did instruct their pupils in some Latin, mathematics, and Greek.

Martin wanted to learn. In the long gray days of winter he bent his head over his books. He tried hard to understand Latin. Latin was the language of the wise and the great. It was the language spoken in the universities and in the church. But when spring warmed the countryside, Martin often glanced up at the open window. He could breathe the moist earth unfolding to the sun. He could see swallows flying northward from the blue skies of Italy.

And then, as he stared out, down on his head would come a heavy blow from a stick, and the teacher would shout harshly, "Martin Luther, stand up! I give you fifteen lashes for laziness." And the leather strap would whistle around his legs.

Often Martin and his friends went home at dusk with sore heads and sore legs. Sometimes punishments would be saved up for several days, and then given out together.

Martin and the other boys paid as little attention to their welts as they could. When school was out, they chased each other down the road toward home. Then the boys would shout, "Sing something, Martin!"

Martin would sing one of the old German songs. And after a while the others joined in. Martin had a fine voice. When the priests found this out, they put him in the choir. He was also sent with a group of boys from house to house to sing for supper for himself and his teacher.

8

One evening Martin said, "Today a new scholar came to teach us. He has been to Rome. Is the pope in Rome the greatest prince, Father?"

"The pope be the great lord of the church, Martin. And the Emperor Maximilian be the great lord of the world."

"But not of all the world, Father. Our teacher says there be a different king of England, and one of France. And there are many lords and princes here in Germany."

"Yea, Martin, and knights and barons too, with their armies and their castles. They rule over us—but above them are pope and emperor."

Then small Martin climbed the stairs and huddled down under his feather cover to dream of princes and popes and knights.

As Martin grew older, there was more to eat at home and a brighter fire on the hearth. Hans Luther was doing better in the mines. He was even planning to buy a smelting furnace of his own. Martin had a warmer jacket and his mother no longer had to bend her back under a load of fagots. They bought wood from the village woodcutter.

Hans was a stern father, and Margaret a strict mother. They punished the children for the smallest offense. Once Martin was whipped by his mother because he took a hazelnut without asking. Yet the parents worked hard to send Martin to school. They saw that this eldest son of theirs had a good mind, and a desire to learn. Already they had decided that he should not work in the mines. Martin must be a great lawyer, and do them honor.

Life in the Luther home was filled with duties. The duty to the church came first. Martin, from his earliest days, was taught

10

that he was constantly watched by a great and just God. But this same God would make lightning strike a boy for any small sin. And Martin came to believe that, no matter how dutifully he lived, in the eyes of God he was always sinful. Only through the help of the Virgin Mary and the saints could he be pardoned. This was taught by the church, and was the belief of all religious people.

The world in which Martin grew up was burdened with fear of evil. Everyone believed that the dark places of the forest were filled with devils and witches. Martin felt that he could almost see the evil one lurking in every shadow. He often heard his mother complaining that the pains in her arms were caused by a witch. She even believed that the witch was one of her neighbors.

But on sunny days Martin laughed and sometimes played pranks on his friends. Singing was always his special delight. Whenever he had a chance to sing, his dark eyes glowed with happiness. And he forgot that he was hungry, or cold, or sinful as his clear voice rose in one of the old Latin chants he had learned in the great stone cathedral.

## A SONG FOR A SUPPER

One evening Hans Luther returned from his work and sat down in his high-backed chair. As he warmed his hands at the fire, he turned to look thoughtfully at his eldest son.

"Martin," said Hans, "you are fourteen now, and well-nigh a man. We should think of other schools. Maybe this one has taught you all that it can teach?"

Martin answered with a laugh, "That happened long since. Now I teach the younger boys, who need help. Thus I keep the whip from their legs."

"So I thought. Now in a few years I can well support your studies in the university. Right now I cannot. These three furnaces I bought are not yet paid for. But I have heard that in Magdeburg there be a school run by the Franciscan monks, where the cost is no more than at the school here. I have been talking to our priest, and to the father of your friend, John Reinicke. John is going to Magdeburg. You may go with him, if you like."

Martin could scarcely keep from shouting in his excitement. How much he could learn in Magdeburg!

A week later the two boys were ready to leave. In the dim light of dawn Martin's mother handed him a small bundle of food for the journey. Behind her stood the younger children, rubbing sleepy eyes. Beside her was Hans, ready for his day at the furnaces.

As he heard John calling outside, Martin had a moment of hesitation. He did not feel that he was "well-nigh a man." How long would it be before he could return to his home? But he lifted his head and said good-by to his father and mother and the children.

Then he marched off beside his friend, his eyes firmly fixed on the way before him.

For a while the two boys said little. Their thoughts were in the homes left behind. But after a time the sun began to warm their faces. They plodded steadily northward, from the borders of the Harz mountains of Thuringia down to level country. Birds sang in the grasses of the fields.

The boys trudged through villages where every hut had a beehive and a pigeon house. But they shuddered at the sight of gallows and stocks in each village. The stocks were wooden pieces to hold a man's arms and legs thrust through holes, so that he could not move. But lifeless bodies hung from the gallows. In the villages belonging to the nobles a peasant could be put in the stocks for days to punish him for stealing a stick of wood. Or a serf could be hung for trapping a rabbit in a noble's forest.

But the day was sunny, and the boys smiled as peasant women in the fields called to them, "God bless you, and a good journey!" When they grew hungry, the boys sat down beside a stream and ate

the bread and cheese from the bundles they carried with them.

Martin and John had to walk fifty miles to get to Magdeburg. Their store of food did not last long. Then they sang for their suppers in the villages they passed through. The villagers smiled and gave them sausage and bread.

Along the way they passed by many other travelers. Martin was amazed at the sight of a fine knight riding a horse jingling with silver trappings. With the knight were ten servants in purple and crimson uniforms. The boys asked an old pilgrim, hobbling along on his stick, about the knight. The ancient man wagged his gray beard as he talked.

"Mayhap that lord be going to see the archbishop," he said. "There be as fine a prince, my lads, as you will see anywhere. The archbishop lives in a palace in Magdeburg. He be so grand that he needs must chew his meat with twelve trumpeters to blow for him."

Sometimes there were so many travelers that Martin and John had to walk beside the road. Carts filled with priests passed them. Merchants trotted by on their horses. Once two Rhinelanders galloped past. They were gay in velvet jackets, plumed hats, and two-colored hose with one leg green and the other striped with yellow.

Martin and John limped wearily into the city of Magdeburg. They were hungry and thirsty. But they stopped often to stare as they wandered about, asking for the monastery. This was a larger city than either of them had ever seen. It was late before they found their way past the high walls to the bleak school building that was to be their home for the next year.

Life with the Franciscan brothers was hard. The school itself had better teachers than the school in Mansfeld. But John and Martin soon found that the pupils were expected to support themselves. So the boys walked about the city begging, or stood in front of a house door to sing for food.

One chilly day Martin, with four other boys, stood shivering on a doorstep. They turned to look at a man who was passing by. He seemed but a skeleton in a monk's robe, bent double under a sack on his shoulders.

"Who is that monk?" asked Martin. "I haven't seen any like him at the monastery."

"Did you not hear," answered John, "of the Prince of Anhalt? He begs for food to give to the hungry. He hopes to reach heaven by doing this." As John whispered, the bent monk peered at them from under his hood, and stumbled slowly away through the streets. Not long after, Martin heard of the death of the Prince of Anhalt. It made a deep impression on him. He thought of this prince as a saintly man.

After a year in Magdeburg, Martin was sent by his parents to

16

a school in Eisenach, where his mother had relatives. Martin walked the fifty miles back to Mansfeld alone. After a brief visit at home, he went on to the city of Eisenach.

Eisenach was a beautiful and a famous place. Looking down on it from a hill was a massive gray stone building called Wartburg Castle. Here gentle Saint Elizabeth had given bread to the poor. Here, it was said, a miracle had taken place. When Elizabeth's cruel husband had forbidden her to feed the poor, bread had been turned into roses to save her from punishment.

In the school at Eisenach Martin had a teacher who was very different from any teacher that he had ever known. This man opened a whole new world of the mind to Martin. In the morning, as the boys sat waiting, Master Trebonius entered, removed his cap, and bowed respectfully to his students.

"Why do you bow to ignorant boys?" asked a friend.

"I am bowing to the future learned men of Germany," the teacher replied.

Martin still earned his bread by singing. He loved to sing, and so went happily, sack in hand, with the other boys.

One evening as Martin trudged from house to house with the boys, they paused before a home on St. George Street, where one of the good families of the town lived. The boys often came here, for Kunz Cotta and his wife never failed to drop a sausage or a loaf of bread or a ripe cheese into each sack. On this day, when the song ended, Martin smiled at the plump and pleasant little woman, who smiled back at him from the open door.

"What is your name, young master?" she asked.

"Martin Luther, by your favor," he answered.

"Then come in and warm yourself, Martin Luther, and all you other boys, too."

The boys walked quietly inside. There a great green tile stove glowed with heat. The room, with its heavy carved furniture, was filled with a smell of roasts and fresh bread.

Before the boys left, Frau Cotta talked with Martin. She learned from his friends, also, how well his teacher thought of him. She invited him to come to see her again. Not long after his first visit, Martin was asked to live with the Cotta family.

From that time Martin was happier than he had ever been in his life. Now he lived in comfort. Frau Cotta saw to it that his cloak was warm and that his cheeks filled out and grew rosy with good food and laughter. Under the sympathetic influence of a real teacher, Martin made rapid progress in his studies. He seemed to leap at the chance to learn. His work was better than that of the other students, and won him the praise of Master Trebonius.

Martin soon made many friends. He could be merry and gay as well as thoughtful and studious. He went with other students to Wartburg Castle. He fished in streams and played games in the

streets. And always he sang. Now his fine voice rose in the church choir. In the evening he delighted to teach the many songs that he knew, happy or sad, to little Henry Cotta, son of his good friends.

For four happy years Martin lived in Eisenach. When it came time for him to attend the famous university at Erfurt, he was sorry to leave.

"Eisenach is my favorite city, and will remain so if I live an hundred years," he said to Frau Cotta.


## COLLEGE DAYS

Martin was eighteen when he went to the University of Erfurt. Hans Luther was proud to be able to support his son in college. The furnaces were making some money for Hans, and he was determined to have his eldest son become a great lawyer. Martin would not have much money to spend in Erfurt, it is true. But he would have enough to keep him comfortably.

The university was a wonderful world to Martin. At first he was much alone, for he did not know any of the other students. He went to board at a dormitory called the Burse of St. George. There he found other students from Thuringia.

Martin Luther was a short, stocky young man, with brilliant dark eyes. He dressed in gay clothing, like the other students. He bought a sword and learned to use it. He wore a cap with a jaunty feather in the side. And, because his voice was often raised in song, he bought a lute and learned to play it. His friends came often to his room to sing and play and to carry on endless discussions.

20

Martin was keenly interested in the subjects he was studying. His professors soon learned that no other student could argue with the clearness and force of Martin Luther. This first year at the university he studied mainly Roman literature and philosophy.

One day Martin was walking with friends in the forest near the Wartburg Castle. They began to sing and to swing their swords in time with the music. Without warning Martin stumbled and fell. He felt a sharp pain in his foot. He had run his sword into it. His friends went for help, and then carried him back to town in a cart. A physician bound the wound. But Martin's foot swelled badly. He became so ill that he expected to die.

As he lay tossing in a fever, Martin opened his eyes and saw an old priest sitting quietly beside him. The priest smiled. He spoke gently, "Be of good comfort, my son; you will not die at this time. God will yet make a great man of you, who will comfort many others."

After some days the fever left, and the wound slowly healed.

Martin again attended his classes. He studied harder than he had ever done before. At the end of his first year at Erfurt University he was able to take his Bachelor of Arts degree.

The next step was the Master of Arts degree. Martin began the more advanced studies which led to this degree. But, while he was interested in these classes, he felt restless. Somehow the gay evenings with his friends, with music and lively talk, were not enough. He spent hours in the library, always searching out new books to read.

Then Martin became aware of the Bible. It lay chained to its stand, almost unused. Not even the students of religion were encouraged to read it. The church itself did not encourage it. But Martin went to the Bible and began to turn over the pages. This was a Bible printed in Latin.

Martin found the story of Samuel and read it through to the end. He was filled with excitement and joy. The great bell clanged for classes. Still Martin stood and read in the Bible.

And when at last he closed it gently and went to his class, he sat there in a daze. His fellow students thought it odd, for Martin was usually eager to argue.

After class, one of his friends walked beside him to his rooms.

"Wherefore, Martin, are you possessed of a blight? Never have I seen you so quiet and so strange."

Martin's eyes lighted and he smiled. "Ah, no, 'tis not a blight indeed. Today I have discovered the Bible. I read of Samuel and his mother, Hannah. I go to church daily, as you know, and I have read books of sermons. Yet much of the Bible is not given to us in church. Of all things on earth I could wish for most, 'tis a Bible of my own."

Two years after his first degree had been granted to him, Martin received his Master of Arts degree. As he stood at the university, in the robe of his master's degree, he thought of the place to which he had come. Through his mind passed scenes of his childhood. Martin remembered his father washing coal dust from his face after a day in the mines or at the furnaces. As if it were yesterday, he could see his mother's back bent under the bundle of fagots. He thought of Frau Cotta and of her gentle, happy

home. She had been a second mother to him. And now he, son of a poor miner, stood here as professors gathered to do him honor.

The procession formed. Behind the professors came the students, singing and laughing. The whole university escorted Martin through the streets of the old town. Merchants and their wives stopped to wave and cheer. Children followed, jumping and calling. Maidservants, hanging feather coverlets from windows, waved and cheered, too.

Now that he had his Master of Arts degree, Martin was entitled to teach. The university offered him a place. At the same time he began his study of law, for it was still his father's wish that he become a great lawyer.

Hans Luther was proud of his son. He addressed Martin respectfully now, when he saw him, as he would a great man.


## A PROMISE KEPT

In 1505, along with the spring, death came to Erfurt. The dreaded black plague was in the town. University classrooms were half empty. As Martin walked through the streets, he saw the fearful black cross of the plague marked upon the door of house after house. Around him he heard the rumble of carts carrying the dead to the cemetery. One of Martin's close friends died just before he was to receive his degree. Like all the others, Martin walked in fear and lay awake at night, listening to the tolling of the bell. But he did not leave the town as so many others did.

By July there was less sickness. Martin longed for the fresh air of the country, for the sights and sounds of home. He decided to walk back to Mansfeld, if only for a few days. As he strode along the highway, he thought of his first journey to Magdeburg, and of his excitement at the new scenes and the strange travelers on the road. Now he was a Master, capped and gowned, and soon to be a lawyer.

The little house in Mansfeld looked smaller and darker than ever. His family were glad to see him, but they greeted him solemnly. Margaret and Hans bowed to him, as if he were already a great man. Martin sat down and drew his lute from his shoulder. He knew how to make them feel at home with him again. Soon he had them all humming and singing, as he played and sang merry student songs. Then, to please his mother, he sang some of the old tunes that he remembered from the days when he had sung for his supper in the town.

On his way back to Erfurt, Martin felt more cheerful. A friar, or wandering monk, walked with him for a time. He told Martin stories of his life on the road. Then, for a few miles, Martin walked with three pilgrims who were returning from Rome. Martin listened to their tales of the holy relics they had seen.

"I touched the toe bone of St. Anthony," said one.

"That be wonderful. I looked upon the veil of St. Veronica."

"And I," said the third, as he hobbled along with the aid of his knobby stick, "I did see a twig of Moses' burning bush."

Martin's thoughts, when the pilgrims had turned into another road, grew gloomy again. The fear of eternal punishment was always with him. The plague had made him conscious of death and had given him a sense of guilt. He felt that he was too

28

sinful to die, if he should be taken. And, truth to tell, he was not overmuch fond of the thought of becoming a lawyer.

Only when he was in church, listening to the swelling beauty of music, was Martin happy. He thought of the Bible, and wished again that he owned one. He thought of his father's gift, presented when he received his degree. He wished it might have been a Bible, instead of an expensive set of law books.

As Martin came near the village of Stotternheim, he saw a dark cloud rising above the horizon. It was thick and thunderous with summer storm. A swift stab of fear darted through him. The world was suddenly a place of terror. He could see the very wrath of heaven in that heavy black cloud. Nearer it came, bringing with it bursts of thunder and sudden flashes of lightning. The cloud was moving directly toward the place where he walked.

Like a bolt of wrath, lightning lashed at the earth close to him. Martin fell headlong to the ground. Surely in such a moment only the saints could save him! He raised his head and cried, "Ah, do but help me, Saint Anne, and I will straightaway become a monk!"

30

Once again lightning flashed near him. Rain came suddenly like a leaden curtain. Martin rose, stood still, and looked about him, as if unaware that rain poured upon him and hail fell clattering on the road.

His cap was crushed flat to his head, and he stood silently in the downpour. Then the rain and hail stopped as suddenly as they had begun. A rainbow arched the distant sky above the village. The sun shone, bright and as if newly made, on the wet and glittering green countryside.

Martin walked slowly toward Erfurt. As he came into the town he smiled and waved to his friends. They called a "Welcome back" to him in return. But somehow the town looked different to him now, for he had made a promise to Saint Anne.

After a few days, when he had thought more about his vow, Martin discussed his plans with his teachers. Then he invited his close friends to his rooms. There, at the close of a gay evening of music and fun, he told them his plans. Quietly he said that he had decided to become a monk.

"Martin," they shouted, "you are jesting!"

"Martin—you a monk? This couldn't be true."

"I have made my choice. I am going into a monastery."

Then the students began to question and argue. It seemed impossible that a man with such a brilliant future should give it all up for the life of a monk.

To enter a monastery meant to give up the world. But the monastery was like a world of its own. Many of them were very wealthy, for their abbots and bishops collected high taxes from peasants living on the large tracts of monastery land. But the wealth went to the church and to the abbots and bishops. The monks lived in stone buildings, called cloisters, where they held masses, worked, and studied. They also went out into the town to help the sick. But they spent much of their time fasting and praying on the cold floors for forgiveness of their sins.

Martin's only thought was to keep his promise to Saint Anne. He wrote to tell his father that he was entering a monastery. The letter he received from old Hans in answer was angry and unforgiving. Hans had counted on having a great lawyer in his family. He had sent his boy to school for that purpose. Now his son was throwing his future away to become a monk. This was sad and bitter news to Margaret and Hans. But they could do nothing about it. Martin would not change his mind.

On joining the monk's order, Martin had to be a beginner, or novice, for a year. During this year he went to prayers seven times daily, rising at the sound of a bell at two o'clock in the morning. At a second bell, he went in his white robe to the church. There the monks were sprinkled with holy water and knelt to pray. Then they took their places in the choir and sang. At the end of the

year Martin took his final vows as a monk, in the monastery of Saint Augustine, at Erfurt. Now he began to study to become a priest. Soon he was ready to say his first mass.

This was a solemn occasion. He invited his father, who had not written to him during the year. Martin was delighted when his father wrote that he would come.

Hans Luther had become a more important man in his village. His furnaces were doing well. He rode to the monastery like a well-to-do man, with a company of twenty horsemen. When he arrived, he made a gift of money to the monastery. After Martin had finished saying his first mass, the whole company was seated at table to celebrate with a feast. Martin sat down beside his father, hoping for some words of forgiveness. "Dear father," he said, "why were you so opposed to my being a monk? The life is so quiet and godly."

The bushy gray eyebrows of the old man drew together

34

angrily. He dropped the piece of bread and meat that he was holding, and jerked his head around. Before all of the monks and learned visitors he shouted, "You learned scholar, have you never read in the Bible that you should honor your father and your mother? And here you have left me and your dear mother to look after ourselves in our old age."

When his father left, Martin went back to his prayers and his work. His work was not easy. Martin was put to scrubbing and sweeping, to begging and to helping the sick. He was given the most disagreeable tasks of the monastery. The other monks thought that he must be proud and arrogant, because he was so well educated. So they tried to make his spirit humble by unpleasant tasks. But Martin surprised them by doing every task willingly. He also fasted more days than were required, and said more prayers.

As he wandered from door to door with his sack on his

shoulder, he sometimes thought of the Prince of Anhalt whom he had seen in his school days in Magdeburg. Martin wondered if he, too, would die young. At night he stretched himself on the cold stone floor of the church and spread out his arms in the shape of a cross. There he stayed so long that he became almost unconscious and had to be helped to bed in his cell.

Martin began to read the Bible a great deal. A large Bible was placed on a stand in the refectory, or dining hall, so that one monk could read aloud from it while the others ate. Martin spent so much time standing before the Bible, reading, that the brothers finally gave him a Bible bound in red leather. Nothing that he had ever received in his life meant so much to him.

Martin was especially interested in the life of Saint Paul, and in his beliefs. He read over and over, "the just shall live by his faith." Jesus began to seem to him to be kind and merciful. And Martin came to believe more and more that faith in Christ would bring forgiveness of sins.

During Martin's third year of his stay in the monastery, Dr. Staupitz, rector of the Augustinian order of monks, came to Erfurt. When he talked with Brother Martin, Dr. Staupitz was surprised at the young monk's unusual knowledge of the Bible. He was also amazed at the learned conversation of this pale, thin monk. He asked the prior of the monastery, who was in charge of the monks, to see that Brother Martin took better care of his health.

On his next visit to the Erfurt monastery Dr. Staupitz made a request. There was a new college in the little town of Wittenberg. He asked that Martin Luther be sent there to teach. The other monks looked at each other and shrugged their shoulders. They

were not surprised. A man who read the Bible and studied so much had no real place in a monastery. He should be in a college.

## ON THE ROAD TO ROME

Not long before Martin went to Wittenberg to teach, Dr. Staupitz sent him on a special mission to Rome. He and another monk from Erfurt were to take a message to the pope.

Martin and his companion set out on foot, toward the south. The road was long, but the two young monks were used to walking. Both of them were filled with a great desire to see Rome, the Holy City. They passed through southern Germany and climbed the Bavarian mountains. Then they trudged over the high Tyrolean pass, and along past beautiful Lake Como and down through Italy. Martin and his friend had no money, but they needed none. At night they stayed at monasteries along the way. And in the morning the monks gave them food for the day.

Italy was completely different from Germany. Both countries were divided into many little kingdoms, but the people of Germany and of Italy had different ways of thinking and living. In both countries there were independent cities and small kingdoms ruled over by princes and nobles. Neither Germany nor Italy were united as nations, as were France, Spain, and England. In Italy, the cities of Florence, Venice, Milan, and Naples had separate rulers, who were often at war with each other. Rome was the city of the pope. He was not only the head of the church, but was also a prince with his own army.

Martin felt at once that Italy was very different from Germany, and difficult to understand. Life was harder in Germany. The people were more serious, and led simpler lives. Here the Italians winked an eye at the most serious beliefs, and often laughed at sacred subjects.

The young northern monks stared in wonder at the great cathedral in Milan, which was still being built. They went with reverence to see the new fresco, "The Last Supper," painted by Leonardo da Vinci in a small chapel on the edge of the city.

Leaving Milan, they crossed the Tuscan mountains and traveled south to Florence. There they saw the palaces of the Medici princes, carved with the lily and the lion, emblems of the great city. In Florence, too, Martin and his friend went to the square where the monk Savonarola had been burned at the stake when he refused to obey the pope.

Beyond Florence, the road to Rome became crowded with pilgrims. They walked, rode, and hobbled along on sticks. As the pilgrims caught their first glimpse of Rome, they fell on their knees in the dusty road. Martin raised his arms and shouted, "Hail, Holy Rome!"

The two monks went to the Vatican palace, the home of the pope. There Martin delivered their message to the pope's secretary, then walked out to see the ancient city. He did not visit the great palaces and public buildings with their wonderful paintings and sculpture. He did not go to see the historic ruins of old Roman days. Instead, Martin went to the churches to pray.

From far-off Germany Martin Luther had always thought of Rome, the Holy City, as a sacred place. Yet as he walked through the dirty streets he could not help but notice the sharp contrast of filth and luxury. Everywhere he saw crime and greed. He passed proud princes and officers of the church dressed in velvet robes, guarded by armed servants. There were paid murderers strolling the streets, and all around there was talk of poisonings and killings. Martin was shocked as he began to realize that Rome was far from holy. It was probably, he thought, the most wicked city in Europe.

On a corner sat a priest selling bones. He was telling people that the bones were relics of saints. In the churches Martin was distressed to hear priests saying mass as fast as possible, and with no reverence at all. And he was disturbed by the stories of the lives of

the popes. The priests who told him these stories only shrugged and said, "Yes, these things are bad — but the popes are all-powerful. They can do as they like."

Martin went to the famous stairway, which the church claimed was the one Jesus ascended on the way to his crucifixion. Like other pilgrims, Martin climbed the stairs on hands and knees, saying prayers and kissing each step. He believed that this act of his would deliver his dead grandfather from the suffering of purgatory. Like other Catholics, he believed that a soul must go to purgatory for a time before reaching heaven.

But when Luther reached the top of the stairway and slowly stood up, he was filled with doubt. Suddenly he spoke aloud, to the surprise of those around him, "Who knows whether it be so?"

As Martin and his friend returned to Germany, the doubt went with Martin. No longer was he able to believe so completely that anyone could save his own soul, or that of another, by doing such things. Slowly he was beginning to believe that it was only by faith in Christ, and by understanding the word of God, as given in the Bible, that a man could find salvation.

After his return from Rome, Martin left the Erfurt monastery and moved to Wittenberg, as Dr. Staupitz had arranged. The little college town was a group of houses on a white sandy hill near the slow-flowing Elbe River. The university, though not so old or important as the one at Erfurt, was under the protection of Frederick the Wise, Prince of Saxony.

It was in the Wittenberg church that Prince Frederick had placed his collection of sacred relics. This was the largest collection in all Germany. Here on the payment of some money, anyone could reduce the church's punishment for his sins, and also reduce his punishment in purgatory. By paying a coin, people could see the tooth of Saint Jerome, hairs from the head of the Virgin Mary, pieces of her cloak, a wisp of straw from Christ's manger, and many other sacred relics. They were all — straw, cloth, hair, or tooth — enclosed in cases of gold and silver. The most valuable was a thorn from the crown of thorns that had encircled the head of Jesus.

Part of the money people paid to see the relics went to help keep up the university where Luther taught. In spite of that, Dr. Luther began to speak against the display of relics. It was even worse, he thought, for the church to permit the selling of slips of paper called indulgences. Anyone who had one of these, signed by the pope, did not have to do the penance demanded by the church for his sins. For a coin a man or woman could buy a pardon for past sins. They could also buy a pardon for the sins of a relative who had died long before.

44

With other monks who taught in the university, Martin
Luther lived in a large stone building called the Black Cloisters.
In the college he lectured on the Bible and on philosophy. In the
hours between lectures he studied in his rooms, or walked in the
cloister gardens. But he spent so much time praying, paid so little
attention to food and sleep, and worried so much over his own
faults that he grew pale and thin and nervous.

One day as Martin Luther sat beneath the pear tree in the
garden, Dr. Staupitz came and sat down beside him. "Brother
Martin," he said, smiling, "I want you to take on a new task.
I would like you to begin to preach."

"Why, I — I could never preach," cried the young monk.
"I do think it would kill me."

"That is quite all right then," answered Dr. Staupitz, with

a twinkle in his eye. "God has plenty of work for clever men in heaven."

Martin laughed and agreed to try. He preached to the monks in the dining hall of the cloisters. Then he became a preacher in the Wittenberg Castle church. This brought him more duties. As a parish priest he had to oversee several monasteries and work with the people. He must hear confessions, visit the sick, comfort those in trouble. And there were many letters to answer. In fact there were so many that Martin said that he could have made use of two good secretaries.

After a while these new duties changed the quiet monk. He was busy getting his ideas down on paper and preparing sermons. He was working out his own beliefs. He was growing more sure of himself, and of what he must teach and preach. Slowly Martin Luther was becoming a leader.

## ON THE CHURCH DOOR

One day three students sauntered towards the castle church, swinging their swords. They were headed toward the church door, which was a kind of bulletin board for college news. Here their professors also placed notices of debates on scholarly subjects. The students wanted to see what new items had been posted there.

The young men drew back respectfully as a short, thin monk, his black robe whipping about his ankles, walked up to the church. In one hand he held a large piece of paper. In the other he carried nails and a hammer.

Placing the paper against the door, the monk nailed it quickly to the wood. Then he turned, nodded pleasantly to the young men, and disappeared toward the university.

"That was Dr. Luther. Look -- "

They read the paper, then stared at each other excitedly. "It's against indulgences! He has posted ninety-five theses against indulgences!"

"That will not please Prince Frederick. He did not like the sermon Dr. Luther preached last year, against the selling of indulgences. And now ninety-five arguments?"

" 'Tis a brave act — this."

A professor came to the door, read the theses slowly and carefully, and went rapidly away. A crowd of students collected. There was much talk. Theses written in Latin and posted on the church door had never attracted such attention before. But this was on a subject that brought forth strong feelings. Germans were growing angry at the way in which the church was allowing indulgences to be sold. Everybody knew that at that moment a well-known seller of indulgences, a monk of bad reputation called Tetzel, was in a nearby town, selling these papers by the thousand. Tetzel carried a huge box, or coffer, with him. Into this, people dropped the money they paid to receive indulgences. A little jingle was being chanted about it:

"As soon as the coin in the coffer rings,
The soul from purgatory springs."

Albert, the archbishop of Mainz, had gotten a big loan from a wealthy German banking company. Now he was collecting money by letting Tetzel and others sell indulgences. Part of this

money would go to pay back the loan and part to help build the great new cathedral of St. Peter's in Rome.

These theses that Martin Luther had nailed on the church door were written by him as subjects for debate. But they were more than that, because Luther was angry. There were three main points in his attack on the selling of indulgences. He said that Germans should not have to pay for the building of St. Peter's in Rome. He said that papal indulgences did not remove guilt. Indulgences were meant to reduce the penance done in this world for sin. But indulgence sellers were telling people that an indulgence brought absolute forgiveness. When Luther heard this, he declared it was not so. Forgiveness must come through faith in Christ, and through feeling sorry for having done wrong. The sinner must also be willing to prove that he was sorry by doing penance. Most important of all, Luther said that buying indulgences would make people feel that being good was not very important. He declared that "he who gives to the poor does better than he who buys an indulgence."

Luther's theses against selling indulgences were printed and sent out through Germany. Not long before Luther's birth, Gutenberg had invented printing by the use of movable type. Because Luther's theses were translated into German and printed, many could read them. Luther had said what many Germans were beginning to think, but had not been able to express clearly.

Martin Luther's voice was now heard far and wide. He had marched in the solemn procession to receive his doctor's degree as a professor, to the tolling of the great bell. He had been presented with the large gold ring and had received the special hat worn by

a professor. He had made a pledge to uphold the truth of the Bible. From distant places now people came to hear his lectures, and to listen to his sermons. The pope in faraway Rome heard that Luther was stirring people up. But he only laughed.

Prince Frederick, the Saxon ruler, wrote Dr. Luther for an explanation. The prince was concerned because these theses brought up problems. If the bankers complained to the pope, and the pope complained to the emperor of Germany, Spain, and the Netherlands — then Prince Frederick might be in trouble with both pope and emperor.

But when Dr. Luther answered, Prince Frederick was impressed. He was sure that this preacher was sincere. From that time on, Prince Frederick protected Luther. Later, when the pope asked to have Martin Luther sent to Rome for trial, Prince Frederick refused to allow him to be taken from Germany.

Martin Luther had defended his views about the indulgences at Augsburg in a debate with Cardinal Cajetan, the pope's representative. The cardinal had ordered Luther to take back what he had declared. As a result of this debate Dr. Staupitz removed Martin Luther from the order of Augustinian monks.

Duke George, cousin of Prince Frederick and ruler of the

other half of Saxony, did not agree with Dr. Luther. He asked him to come to Leipzig for a public debate with Dr. John Eck, defender of the right to sell indulgences and of the views of the Roman church.

In July, 1519, Luther rode the forty miles to Leipzig in a country cart, seated on straw. This debate was an important event. People took sides either with Martin Luther or with Dr. Eck. Some of them believed in indulgences, and some did not. Both Dr. Luther and Dr. Eck were afraid that the people might form mobs and attack them. But this did not keep Luther from going to Leipzig, the chief city in Duke George's part of Saxony.

With Dr. Luther went some friends. Philip Melanchthon, a fellow professor, rode in the cart beside Luther. Melanchthon was a thin young man who looked as if a good breeze from the Harz mountains could blow him away. But when he stood at the desk and lectured, none who listened thought of his frail body, but only of the strength of his mind and spirit. Nearly two hundred students walked beside and behind the cart, armed with battle-axes to protect Dr. Luther.

As the group from Wittenberg came into the crooked streets of the old city of Leipzig, they heard music. A guard was marching with Duke George's banners, to music of fife and drum. With this guard walked Dr. Eck, in his professor's robe and hat. He was accompanied also by his own company of seventy-six men.

Next day the men from Wittenberg went to the castle. There they entered the great hall, already filled with counts, knights, professors, and townsmen. Martin Luther stepped forward to meet the great Dr. Eck, who was to give the views of the pope in Rome.

All sorts of arguments were offered by Dr. Eck to prove that Martin Luther was offering false religious beliefs. But Luther could answer them all. Then Dr. Eck cleverly brought up the ideas of John Hus. Hus was a religious leader who had been burned to death many years before in Bohemia, for disagreeing with some of the beliefs of the church. Dr. Eck drew from Luther the statement that not all of the opinions of Hus were wrong. This brought a gasp of horror from the crowd. The Duke frowned and tapped his fingers angrily on the arm of his chair. He was certain now that Luther was a heretic — one who did not agree with the church beliefs.

When the discussion ended, Luther and his party went back to Wittenberg. The professors were silent. The students whispered among themselves in dismay. Everyone expected trouble to follow.

And trouble did follow. During the next summer the pope, Leo, signed a paper called a bull. This said that if Martin Luther had not changed his opinions within sixty days he would be cast out of the church. In November, a representative of the emperor burned Luther's books in a public bonfire in the city of Cologne.

Luther's friends talked often of all this. What would come of it? There was danger that Luther would be burned as a heretic, as John Hus had been. The Wittenberg students could talk of little else. They neglected their studies to discuss it. What would Dr. Luther do?

Then, on a chilly December morning, a crowd of students gathered about the door of the castle church. On the door a notice was fastened.

"Read it aloud, Adolph. You are close enough. You are

54

almost pushing the paper through the door. Read it!"

The student's voice rose, loud and clear: "Let whoever believes in the truth of the Gospel be present at ten o'clock this morning, outside the Elster Gate. There the impious books of papal decrees and theology will be burned, inasmuch as the boldness of the enemies of the Gospel has waxed so great that they daily burn the books of Luther. Come, pious and zealous youth — "

Slowly the students and professors gathered at the university, talking quietly. The door opened, and out strode Dr. Luther. He went straight to the gate, then waited while the professors and students moved into a procession behind him.

As the solemn crowd moved toward the outskirts of the town, folk gathered in the streets to watch and to wonder. This was something unheard of. They crossed themselves, and prayed that good Dr. Luther might never be taken to another fire, in Rome.

Outside the city walls, beyond the Elster Gate, a bonfire was already laid. One of the teachers struck spark from a flint, and the flames leaped in the dry fagots.

No one spoke as Dr. Luther stepped forward. He placed on the fire the books of Canon Law. These were the laws that told the powers of the pope over all priests, churches, and people. Then Dr. Luther drew forth the pope's bull casting him from the church. This, too, he laid on the fire. The flame took the paper, curled it instantly, and sent it flying upward, a gray wisp of ash. Dr. Luther raised his powerful voice and spoke, and everyone understood that his words were directed to the pope himself:

"Because thou hast brought down the truth of God, he also brings thee to this fire today. Amen."

Luther bowed his head. The men and boys did so, too. Then the teachers returned to the university. For a while the students paraded around the fire, singing. As the flames died away, they went back to town. As they marched, they sang a hymn. Before them, on the point of a sword, they held up an indulgence paper.

Dr. Luther continued to teach and preach. But now he spent much of his time sitting at his heavy table, goose quill in hand,

writing. During the summer of 1519, he had published several pamphlets. As soon as Dr. Luther's books and pamphlets were finished, they were printed in German and sent out to all parts of the country.

In other sections of Germany — Thuringia, the Rhineland, and up to the North Sea, as well as in Saxony — Germans were reading the strong words of Martin Luther.

## "HERE I STAND"

On the death of Emperor Maximilian in 1519, Charles V became Emperor of the Holy Roman Empire. This was a group of European kingdoms whose princes were subject to the emperor. They also elected him to his office. Charles was the grandson of Ferdinand and Isabella of Spain on his mother's side, and was a member of the ruling family of Germany on his father's side.

In the year 1521, Charles V called together his first gathering of princes at the city of Worms, on the Rhine River in Germany. This meeting was known as the Diet, and the emperor considered that its rulings were absolute law. One of the problems before the Diet was what to do about the rebellious professor of Wittenberg. It was decided to bring Luther to trial at the Diet to be held at Worms.

In April, 1521, Dr. Luther received a summons to appear before the Diet. His friends advised him not to go. But Luther said he had been summoned by the emperor and that he would be there. He knew, though, that he was in danger of being captured

59

and taken by force to Rome to stand trial before the pope. So he waited until he received a pledge of safe conduct from the emperor.

When the royal herald arrived with the safe conduct, Martin Luther climbed into a cart and headed for Worms. Three of his friends went with him. They were Dr. Amsdorf, Peter Swaven, and John Petzensteiner. In front of the cart rode the emperor's royal herald, Caspar Sturm. He carried high the imperial banner with its black two-headed eagle and the royal coat of arms on a yellow silk background.

As the cart rattled along the muddy road, Martin drew out his lute. Plucking the strings softly, he began to sing. Dr. Amsdorf looked at him in surprise.

"And you can sing, Martin, when your very life is in danger?"

Dr. Luther smiled, and sang on. After a while Amsdorf was humming, too, and soon they all joined in. The herald, riding stiffly before the cart, turned his head to stare.

"What manner of man is this Luther, then — that he can sing when the pope and the emperor join forces against him?"

As they passed through the city of Leipzig, people flocked into streets to see Martin Luther. At Weimar, Justus Jonas, another good friend of Luther, jumped into the cart to go along.

In Erfurt they were greeted by music. It sounded as if the whole town sang to Martin Luther. Luther's dark eyes gleamed when he saw that the students and professors, headed by the rector himself, had come in a procession to greet him.

That night the town officials gave a banquet in Luther's honor. Afterward he and his friends slept in the monastery — the same monastery of St. Augustine where he had once lived.

Next day was Sunday. Dr. Luther preached in the church
where he had been choir boy. So many crowded in that the balcony
creaked and groaned under their feet.

As the cart proceeded westward on its journey, Luther's
friends came from towns and villages to warn him that his life was
in danger. They told him that he should not go on. But Martin
Luther only smiled a little. "I shall go to Worms," he said to them,
"though there were as many devils there as tiles on the roofs."

As they approached the city, Luther saw that crowds lined
the road. People smiled and cheered him.

Martin Luther stepped from his cart with wisps of straw

clinging to his robe. With his lute under his arm he said firmly, "God will be with me." Then he strode into the doorway of the place where he was to stay — the house of the Knights of St. John.

Until late at night Dr. Luther had no rest, for crowds of visitors came to talk with him. On Wednesday morning he prepared for his appearance before the Diet. But he found time to give the last sacrament to a dying Saxon knight who had asked for his prayers.

That afternoon, at four o'clock, the royal herald and the imperial marshal came to escort Dr. Martin Luther to the Diet. Luther walked quietly, but with firm steps, to the great hall in the bishop's palace. He waited for two hours outside the hall. When he entered at six o'clock, it was dark. Torches were burning in sconces along the walls.

The great hall was packed. Along the walls stood lines of Spanish and German soldiers. The emperor, Charles V, was a young man of twenty years. He sat on his throne, clad all in black except for a large jewel glittering about his neck. Around him were the six princes, electors of the empire, and the representatives of the pope. There were bishops and ambassadors and knights.

All eyes were fixed on the quiet man as he entered. If the power of the pope were to be maintained, Martin Luther must submit to it and admit that he had been wrong.

An official came forward and told Luther that he was to say nothing, but only to answer questions. Martin Luther drew his heavy eyebrows together in a frown. His questioner was a Dr. Eck, but not the same Dr. Eck with whom he had debated at Leipzig.

Dr. Eck stepped forward. He pointed to a pile of books and pamphlets on a table. He asked if Dr. Luther had written these books, and if he would admit that he had been wrong in the opinions put into them? Luther said nothing. Slowly, one by one, the titles of the books were read aloud. Then Dr. Luther spoke. He said that they were his books, and that he had written others, too. Then he asked for time to consider Dr. Eck's question. Dr. Eck spoke to the emperor, who gave Luther one day.

All that night Luther prayed. Next day his anxious friends were surprised to find him in good spirits, laughing and joking. Again at four he was escorted to the large hall. Again he stood on trial before the assembly of great men.

64

This day Luther spoke for some time in German. He spoke of his writings, and what they meant. The hall was hot and stuffy with smoke from the torches on the walls. As he stopped speaking, Luther looked exhausted. He was asked to repeat all that he had said in Latin. At this a knight cried out, "If you can't do it, doctor, you've done enough."

But Dr. Luther took a deep breath and repeated his statement in Latin. When he finished, Dr. Eck shouted, "Luther, you have not answered to the point. Will you take back what you have written, or not?"

Martin Luther raised his head. His eyes blazed, and his voice echoed to the ends of the hall. He said simply:

"I cannot and will not recant anything, for it is neither safe nor right to act against one's own conscience. Here I stand. I cannot do otherwise. God help me. Amen."

On Friday, Martin Luther left Worms. His safe conduct was

¹ for twenty days. He had not given in to the pope. But
᠁zed with rumors. Plots were being whispered from
᠁e. Luther's friends were anxious about him. Would
᠁ourney home? If the emperor should withdraw
᠁many were trying to get him to do, Luther
᠁he road by hired killers. Would he be safe
᠁He had been condemned by both church
᠁᠁ as if he could not escape being taken to Rome
᠁efore the pope, which meant death by burning.

᠁the journey back from Worms was as pleasant as the
co᠁᠁ng had been. Peasants left their fields to wave to Luther. In
towns and villages he was met by cheering merchants and students
and housewives. He stopped to preach in several places, then went
to the village of Mohra. There he rested for several days at the
home of his uncle.

On the fourth of May, Martin Luther climbed once more
into his cart and rode toward Wittenberg. As he passed from the
village of Mohra, he looked up to watch the long-legged storks
solemnly guarding their young in nests on rooftops. He saw the
young rye sprouting in the fields and smelled freshly turned earth,
damp from spring rains. A pear tree blossoming by the roadside
reminded him of the garden of the Black Cloisters in Wittenberg.
He would be glad to be home again.

The cart bounced and rolled along the rough road into a
forest. In the deep shade of old trees arching over the roadway
there was the song of birds. Martin was almost asleep in the straw.
A sudden noise of horses' hoofs made him sit up in alarm. A

troop of armed men dashed from among the trees. The frightened
driver of the cart pulled up and stopped.

"Ho, there! Halt!"

The horsemen surrounded the cart. The leader called out, "Be
you Dr. Luther, of Wittenberg?"

"Yes," replied Luther quietly, but with a pale face. "What do
you wish of me?"

"Mount this horse, sir, and come with us."

Dr. Luther was helped from the cart, and to the back of a
saddled horse. The armed leader shouted to the driver of the cart to
return to the village. Then away the men galloped, taking Luther
with them. As he turned to catch a last glimpse of his terrified

friends, Luther thought that now he was about to die. But the horses sped through a countryside that gradually became familiar. Wasn't that a cottage near Erfurt where he had once taken shelter when, as a student, he had been caught in a rainstorm? Why—those grim stone towers must surely belong to Wartburg Castle?

As he clattered across the drawbridge and heard the gate come down, closing the entrance behind him, Luther began to smile. This castle, he knew, was not filled with enemies. Inside the court-yard he was greeted respectfully and made welcome. Then he was escorted to his rooms.

Luther soon found out that Prince Frederick had arranged for him to be kidnaped. Here in the castle he was to be a prisoner for his own safety. He was disguised as a knight, and was called Junker George.

So Luther cast off his robe and brown cap and dressed as a knight. He wore a thick gold chain about his neck and he carried

a sword. He let his hair grow long and grew a beard. He must act like a knight, too. That meant, among other things, hunting. But Dr. Luther did not like hunting and he joined a stag hunt only when requested.

All over Germany there was a great uproar. The famous artist of Nürnberg, Albrecht Dürer, wept when he heard of the kidnaping of the Wittenberg professor. Luther wrote to a few friends to tell of his safety, but at first he did not say where he was hidden. Most people thought him dead.

There at Wartburg Castle Dr. Luther settled down to a quiet and a lonely life. He was restless, for he felt that he ought to be out in the world, protesting against the wrongs practiced by those who controlled the church. Instead, he rode in the forest, walked up and down the castle courtyard, or sat at a great table, writing.

## "FROM THE MIDST OF THE BIRDS"

Martin Luther lived in Wartburg Castle as Junker George for a year. He watched the summer come. He strolled in the fields, seeing the birds nesting in the grasses and the young leaves growing dark green on the trees. He wrote letters to his friends, dating them "from the regions of the air" or "from the midst of the birds, which sing sweetly on the branches of the tall trees, and praise God, night and day, with all their might." He saw the harvests in autumn, with the gathering of the fruit. When the wind blew cold and snow drifted down on the castle, he stayed close to his fire in the big high-ceilinged room till the storm was over.

71

All this time Luther wrote pamphlets and sent them to Wittenberg to be printed and sold. People throughout Germany read them with joy, for they knew that this meant that Dr. Luther still lived, and wrote for them. Luther then began to do something that he had long wanted to do but for which he had not found time. He began to translate the New Testament into German. The German language differed in different parts of the country. But Luther thought he could use a kind of German that all could understand.

For many months Luther toiled at this task. By day he sat at a table near a high and narrow window. Through its small, leaded panes of green glass the light came in as if through water. By night he worked with two candles on his table and a fire on the hearth.

One night, when Dr. Luther had worked long, he felt restless and unhappy. He tried to go on with his task. But the flickering fire cast strange shadows before him on the wall. He was very

tired, and had had little sleep. Still, he felt he must get on with this important work.

Suddenly Luther looked up and saw a black shadowy shape before him in the dim room. In Germany at this time everyone felt that devils and witches were often near, and sometimes people thought they saw them. That shape, Luther was sure, was the devil watching him. Grasping the first weapon handy to him—it was his big inkpot—he threw it with all his strength at the devil. The inkpot thudded against the wall. Martin drew his hand across weary eyes and went to bed.

Next morning on the floor he saw his inkpot, and on the wall a great splash of ink. He refilled the inkpot, took up his pen, and returned to work on his translation of the Bible.

At last Martin Luther finished his work of translating the New Testament. Now he was receiving answers to his letters to his friends in Wittenberg. These held disturbing news. His friends told him that indulgences were still being sold throughout the country. They wrote that Dr. Luther was permanently under the ban of both church and state. The state supported the church. The church would not permit any of its beliefs to be questioned or its orders defied. Anyone who gave him food, clothing, or shelter was threatened with punishment. People were also forbidden to read any of his writings. Germans were divided into those who believed in Luther and his views, and those who sided with the pope and emperor against him.

Two warlike knights were ready to fight for the new cause, although Luther did not approve of armed rebellion. And some professors who called themselves followers of Luther urged doing away with monasteries and nunneries. They also wished to remove some of the old forms and ceremonies of the church. Some of Luther's followers went so far as to destroy images in churches and other church property.

Dr. Luther did not like such changes. He had raised his voice to condemn some practices of the church that he considered wrong.

Martin Luther thought about all of these things constantly. He was concerned about removing the false doctrines of the church. He saw that many things that people had taken for granted were doing harm. But he was afraid of the violent actions some of his followers were beginning to consider. He did not want to go to such lengths to change the church ritual.

When Luther received a letter from Philip Melanchthon asking him to return to Wittenberg, he decided to go. He sent an urgent request to Prince Frederick asking for release from Wartburg Castle. The prince thought it dangerous and unwise, but let Luther decide for himself. Still wearing a beard and clothed as a knight, Dr. Luther left the castle for Wittenberg.

At Jena, on his road home, "Junker George" sat one evening in the Black Bear Inn. He was reading as he ate his supper. At the sound of newcomers at the door, he glanced up. Two young students in Swiss dress entered. The stout innkeeper hurried to them.

"Come in, young sirs. A joint be turning on the spit at the fire and will be ready soon for your supper."

"We will sit here by the door," said one of the students, "for we are muddy from our long tramp."

"Junker George" smiled and called to them heartily, "Come join me here. 'Twill be a blessing to have good conversation."

As the students approached, Luther heard the innkeeper whisper to them, " 'Tis Luther, the monk, who tweaks the very nose of the pope."

But the students saw only a black-bearded man in red hose and a knight's attire. They stared at the innkeeper, thinking that he had, perhaps, had too much of his own ale.

When supper had been eaten, both young men were amazed at the brilliant talk of the strange knight. On the table beside him was a book containing the Hebrew Psalter. And the knight talked not of dogs and deer, but of the Gospel.

"We are on our way to the University of Wittenberg," said the taller student. "Word has spread that Dr. Luther is alive and safe. But do you know whether he be in Wittenberg?"

"I know that he is not now, but soon will be," replied the knight with a laugh. "And if you call on Dr. Jerome Schurf there, say to him that he who is to come sends greetings."

The students nodded but frowned. This knight—he was very odd indeed. Luther did not see the young men again. He left on his horse at dawn. When he reached Wittenberg, he went straight to the home of Dr. Schurf. There he received a joyful greeting from his friends, Justus Jonas, Nicholas Amsdorf, and Melanchthon.

As they sat talking, rejoicing in Luther's return home, there was a timid knock on the door. When the door was opened, the Swiss students came in. As they saw the knight, they looked so amazed that Dr. Luther roared with laughter. He called out to them that Dr. Luther had returned indeed. Then he introduced them to some of their future professors.


## A WEDDING

Once again Martin Luther lived in the Black Cloisters. His days were very full. He lectured at the university and preached in the great church, and people continued to come from near and far —even from other countries—to hear him.

At night, when quiet settled around the old monastery, Luther would sit at his table, writing. His quill pen sped across the pages. The printing presses were busy getting out copies of his pamphlets and books to be sent out over Germany.

All the world was restless and troubled. This was a time of

change. New ideas and adventures were opening up. The Middle Ages were giving way to the beginning of the modern world.

Explorers were sailing farther and farther out from Europe. Columbus' discovery of America, nine years after Luther's birth, had been followed by Pizarro's venture into South America. Cortez had conquered Mexico and shipped golden treasure to Spain. World trade followed the explorers. These voyages were made possible by the invention of the mariner's compass. And the conquest of strange lands came with the use of guns and gunpowder.

The telescope was making secrets of the skies known to man. The invention of the printing press and use of engraving made it possible to spread ideas over Europe. More and more people were learning to read. In Italy great pictures were being painted, and in Germany Albrecht Dürer was painting and engraving woodcuts. The old Greek writings were translated and published. Learned scholars, such as Erasmus in Holland, wrote books that were read in many countries.

But the peasants who worked in the fields were hungry. They had to pay very high taxes to the nobles and the abbots and bishops of the monasteries. These churchmen lived like princes on their estates. Peasants revolted against the nobles and monasteries from time to time, when crops failed and taxes were very high. Then Roman laws were brought into Germany. These laws gave lands, forests, and waters that had been used by all of the peasants, to nobles as private property. When the peasants rioted, the nobles punished them cruelly. A man could be put to death for stripping the bark from a tree in a noble's forest. The riots spread to the cities.

During the Middle Ages knights and barons fought constantly against each other. To stop this, the ruling princes made laws forbidding armed fighting. This threw professional soldiers out of work, and they took to highway robbery. Merchants were growing richer, and both the knights and the peasants resented this prosperity. When crops failed, peasants took to roaming the roads, joining great crowds of beggars. The whole countryside became dangerous. Castles and monasteries were robbed and burned. Church property was sometimes destroyed.

When Dr. Luther first heard of these riots, his sympathies were with the hungry peasants, but later, at news of riot and bloodshed, he grew angry. Martin Luther had never before approved of

violence. But now he published a pamphlet advising the nobles to use violence to put down the riots of the peasants. This pamphlet made the peasants so angry that many of them turned against him, and left his religious movement. Later, when the nobles had been cruel in their attacks on the peasants, Luther wrote that the devils that had entered the peasants had gone into the victors, instead of going back to hell.

Martin Luther was blamed by the pope and Catholic high churchmen for starting the peasant revolt. Actually, Luther never intended to do anything but reform some of the teachings of the church he felt were false.

But as Luther saw the old church forms breaking, his own

83

ideas on some of them began to change. When he had first returned to Wittenberg he was displeased to find that monks and nuns were leaving their convents. Sometimes they married and returned to ordinary life in the towns. Luther gradually began to believe that a priest could marry and still be a minister to his people. His own friends, professors and scholars, were getting married. Philip Melanchthon was married and had a pleasant home in Wittenberg. Some of these friends urged Luther to marry also. Several wealthy girls were suggested to him, but he refused to consider changing his way of life.

Not far from the town of Grimma there was a convent where for generations daughters and sisters of nobles had entered to become nuns. When the new religious ideas began to spread, twelve of these nuns decided to leave. They wrote to Dr. Luther to ask his help. Luther asked a friend who had business dealings with the convent to arrange for the nuns to escape so they could return to their homes.

Luther's own home, the Black Cloisters, was almost deserted now. Most of the monks had put aside their vows and gone out into the world.

One night Dr. Luther heard a knocking on the big wooden door. He got up and went to answer it. There before the doorway was a country wagon, and climbing down from it were nine nuns. Luther was so amazed that at first he could only stand and stare.

The nuns, like dark shadows in their robes, peered up at him from white headdresses.

"Can you find shelter for us, Dr. Luther?" asked one of them. "Only three of us could go home. What shall we do?"

Luther had not thought of such a problem as this. But he held the door wide. "You shall have shelter here. I will try to provide help for you."

When he had given the nuns some of the monks' vacant cells, Dr. Luther sat down in his room to think. These girls knew nothing of life outside the convent walls. Indeed he must help them. He picked up his pen and drew some paper toward him. That night he wrote to his friends as well as to friends and relatives of the nuns.

Soon offers of help began to arrive. Relatives of some of the nuns came or sent for them and took them home. From citizens of the towns around came offers of marriage for others. A friend of Luther's, Lucas Cranach, and his wife offered to take two of the girls into their home until other places could be found for them. Cranach was the artist who had illustrated many of Luther's pamphlets.

After a while there was only one nun left to be helped. Her

name was Katherine von Bora. Luther asked a lawyer friend and his wife to take Katherine into their home.

Katherine von Bora was not a beautiful girl, but she was energetic and intelligent. After a time Dr. Glatz, rector of Wittenberg University, asked her to marry him. Dr. Amsdorf—a bachelor like his friend Martin Luther—asked Katherine whether she would marry Dr. Glatz. Katherine replied, "I will marry nobody but you, Dr. Amsdorf, or Dr. Luther himself."

When Amsdorf told Luther of this remark, Luther laughed and thought it a joke. Martin Luther did not intend to marry at all. He knew that many would criticize him for marrying, since he had been a monk. Marrying a girl who had been a nun would be especially talked about, and might hurt his cause. He knew, too, that he might have to die for his beliefs, and he thought that a man who was in constant danger of being burned at the stake would not make a good husband.

But when he came to know Katie von Bora better, Luther

87

began to believe that he had been wrong. He talked it over with his father. Old Hans was pleased at the thought of having his son marry, and advised him to do it. Luther made up his mind to go ahead, but told only three of his friends of his plans. The wedding was simple. It took place on June 13, 1525, in the evening. To Luther's disappointment, Philip Melanchthon would not come to the marriage ceremony, for he did not approve of it.

Martin and Katie lived in the Black Cloisters, the place that had been Martin's home ever since he first came to Wittenberg. It was a large building, and though the monks who once lived there had left long since, it still sheltered wandering monks who passed

88

by. For a wedding present, Prince Frederick gave Luther the Black Cloisters, and it became the home of the Martin Luther family.


## UNDER THE PEAR TREE

The Luther household was a happy one. Katie was a good wife. She worked hard and managed well, and soon had the dirt and disorder of a bachelor house cleared up. She served good meals, and saw to it that her husband's clothing was mended properly. She also managed, after a while, to save enough money to buy a small farm, though Luther's salary as a professor was small. Martin Luther laughed at his wife's businesslike ways and called her "My lord, Katie." But he grew very fond of her, and was glad to have her take him in hand so well.

Katie often scolded her husband for giving away so much money and food. "Martin," she cried, standing in the doorway of his study with hands on hips, "you would give away our last loaf to any thieving beggar. Why, only yesterday, I saw a stranger leaving here in your best cloak. We must live, too, you know."

Then she hid the remaining money in her clothespress. As her rage mounted, she went to the kitchen and hid the freshly baked loaves too. Martin promised to do better—but he forgot his promise again when a needy man knocked at his door. About this time a friend of Dr. Luther received a letter from him, saying, "I am sending you a vase as a wedding present. P.S.—Katie hid it."

Dr. Luther was sometimes reproved by friends for his liking for gaiety. He liked pictures and theatricals, and he relished a good

meal with interesting companions. Most of all he loved music. Playing the lute and singing were among his greatest joys.

Katie usually had several students as well as nieces and nephews boarding with them in the Black Cloisters. The house was filled with visitors coming and going. At the long dining table there was enough, in spite of a rather lean purse, for twenty-five people. The table talk was so lively that some of the students wrote it down from day to day as their host spoke.

Sometimes Dr. Luther talked of himself, and of his father and his mother. He said, "I am the son of a peasant, and the grandson and the great-grandson. My father wanted to make me into a lawyer. He went to Mansfeld and became a miner. I became a scholar. Then I became a monk and put off the student cap. My father didn't like it, and then I annoyed the pope and married a nun. Who could have read that in the stars?"

As the years passed, six children were born to Martin and Katie Luther. This delighted old Hans and Margaret Luther. Their first grandson was named Hans. Dr. Luther wrote in his journal, "Hans is cutting his teeth and beginning to make a joyous nuisance of himself." Then came Elizabeth, Magdalena, named for her Aunt Lena who lived with them, and young Martin. Paul

and Margaret were the youngest children. Elizabeth died when she was a baby, and the death of Magdalena at the age of fourteen saddened Martin and Katie Luther. But the children added much joy to the big household, and filled the Black Cloisters with laughter and song.

Of a summer's evening, when the light of the setting sun touched the roses and lilies, the family gathered in the garden. They sat under the old pear tree. Dr. Luther proudly pointed out to them each new blossom on the flowers that he had planted, and called to Hans to keep the frisky dogs off. Then, after some lively games with the children, Dr. Luther sat on a bench and picked up his lute. The children thought this was the best time of all. Their father's voice rose in one of the hymns that he had written himself. When they heard their mother singing, they joined in, too:

"A mighty fortress is our God,
A bulwark never failing;
Our helper he, amid the flood
Of mortal ills prevailing."

"That's a fortress like the Wartburg Castle, where you lived as Junker George, isn't it, Father?" called out Paul.

Luther smiled. He stopped singing to tell his children of his life in the big stone castle, and of the hunts and the deep snows of winter. And then he talked of his own childhood, and of his parents, who had worked so hard to send him to school.

Hans and Margaret Luther were dead now, but Martin Luther's brothers still lived in and around Mansfeld. Dr. Luther promised his children that some day they might visit their cousins in Thuringia.

## FATHER OF THE REFORMATION

As Martin Luther grew older, his health began to fail. He had frequent headaches. He was also saddened by news of some of his followers being put to death because they refused to give up their Lutheran beliefs. But Dr. Luther never stopped working for long. He preached in many towns and lectured in the University of Wittenberg. He traveled from church to church, and wrote many letters and pamphlets. He translated the Old Testament, and completed his work on the Bible. He wrote hymns as well as books and pamphlets, and would take no pay for them.

The family income was increased, however, by gifts of food and clothing from friends as well as from Prince John. Prince John, who had become Elector of Saxony on the death of his brother Prince Frederick the Wise, helped Martin Luther in every way possible. Prince John was an active supporter of the new and growing Lutheran church.

The Lutheran church movement was spread through Germany by pamphlets and by storytelling cartoons. Luther wrote hundreds of these booklets. Artists and printers risked their lives

to work on them. Catholics printed pamphlets against Lutherans, but not in such quantities.

The Lutheran religious movement came to be accepted in most of north Germany, as well as in the important cities of the south. Town officials would not forbid Lutheran church services in places where this would cause trouble.

At first there was confusion in the churches. Then the German princes decided that all the people in each district must follow the religion of its prince. If the prince became a Lutheran, all the people and priests in his district must become Lutherans or move to a Catholic district. The Lutheran churches in each district were headed by its prince, and run by a group of scholars and judges.

As Martin Luther's health grew worse, he found it impossible to work in the mornings. So he spent more time with his family and the students, and less time traveling. But he continued to preach and write. Wittenberg was now a large town, filled with people who came to hear Dr. Luther. He found it a difficult task to answer his letters, for he received so many. But he did answer most of them.

In January of the year 1546, Dr. Luther went to Eisleben, the town in which he had been born sixty-three years before. His three sons went with him. The boys went on from there to Mansfeld to have their long-promised visit with their cousins. Dr. Luther went to stay in the home of his old friend, the town clerk. That day a cold wind was sweeping through Eisleben from the mountains. It rattled the roof tiles and seemed to snatch at Dr. Luther's head and neck with icy fingers as he got stiffly down from the cart in which

he had traveled. Luther felt ill, but he attended to the business that had brought him to Eisleben, and he remained there several weeks.

On the Sunday of Saint Valentine's Day Dr. Luther, though not well, went to preach in the church where he had been baptized. That day he wrote a letter to Katie. He told her he planned to leave for home on February 18.

But the night before he was leaving, he was taken seriously ill. His sons came at once from Mansfeld. As his children and friends stood about his bed, Dr. Jonas asked, "Reverend Father, do you stand firm by Christ and the doctrine you have preached?"

Martin Luther opened his eyes and in a strong voice said, "Yes."

A short time later he passed away.

Martin Luther was buried in the Wittenberg Castle church, near the tomb of his protector, Prince Frederick. The largest crowd ever to gather in the town came for his funeral.

That night Wittenberg was in mourning. Everyone there spoke of Dr. Martin Luther. In cities, towns, and villages all over Germany, people spoke of Martin Luther. Many things were said of him, both good and bad, by Lutherans and by Catholics. All called him a brave man. Lutherans said that he had had the courage to speak out against the acts and beliefs he considered wrong within the church. Catholics said that he, who had been a monk, had sinned in marrying a girl who had been a nun.

But many Germans knew that here, for the first time, was a pastor who had had a home life like other men, and whose home was a good example to other citizens. Parents taught Luther's catechism to their children, and they all sang the hymns written by Luther. In many homes of Germany, then and ever since, Luther's Bible has been read to families sitting by the fire or in the gardens under their fruit trees. It played an important part in the development of the German language. Martin Luther came to be called the Father of the Reformation, and the man who made possible the formation of the Protestant churches.